SCHIRMER'S LIBRARY OF MUSICAL CLASSICS

Vol. 1489

ROBERT SCHUMANN

Op. 46

Andante and Variations

For Two Pianos

Edited by

EDWIN HUGHES

(Two copies required for performance)

ISBN 0-7935-5205-2

G. SCHIRMER, Inc.

DISTRIBUTED BY

HAL•LEONARD®
CORPORATION

7777 W. BLUEMOUND RD. P.O. BOX 13819 MILWAUKEE, WI 53213

T0051119

Andante and Variations

For Two Pianos

Edited by
Edwin Hughes

R. Schumann. Op. 46
Composed in 1843

Ped. simile

Ped. simile

dim.

dim.

Più animato ♩ = 116

Più animato ♩ = 116

Ped. simile

14

Ped. simile

Ped. simile